Granny in her kitchen, 1990s.

From GRANNY'S Kitchen

A glimpse into the kitchen of a woman we will never forget.

A Compilation By
Kaylin R. Adkins

Edited By Geraldine K. Perry and Earlene K. Adkins
Published by Hourglass Omnimedia, LLC
Huntington, WV

Hourglass Omnimedia, LLC
Huntington, WV

This book is a compilation of recipes collected from Wanda Violet Adkins Wooten Dean's (known more publicly to everyone as 'Granny') personal archives. These recipes are from Granny, as well as from her family and friends. Any resemblance to other recipes from persons, living or dead, is entirely coincidental.

The intellectual property (recipes, stories, photographs, and all related content) contained within this book is protected by Hourglass Omnimedia, LLC.

Copyright © 2016 by Hourglass Omnimedia, LLC / Kaylin Renee Adkins

All rights reserved. Reproduction of this book in its entirety is prohibited. Recipe reproduction may be copied on a case-by-case basis, with permission from the publisher. Recipes are to be used for personal use only and cannot be sold.

First Hourglass Omnimedia, LLC paperback edition 2016.

All proceeds of this book, if any, will be donated to a nonprofit organization related to hospice care, stroke prevention/research, or another association approved by Granny's family.

Print ISBN 978-0-9968233-0-2
eBook ISBN 978-0-9968233-2-6

Library of Congress Control Number 2016912348

Manufactured in the United States of America.

www.hourglassomnimedia.com
www.kaylinadkins.com

Four generations, 2015: Granny, Geraldine, Earlene, Kaylin.

"A heart is not judged by how much you love, but how much you are loved by others."— **The Wizard in "The Wizard of Oz,"** 1939.[1]

This book is dedicated to the woman who forever changed my life—my beautiful Guardian Angel, my Granny Wanda Violet Adkins Wooten Dean. You are always in our hearts and in our genetics. I hope at least some of you rubbed off on me. I'm proud to be part of your lineage and your legacy. I was honored on Earth to be part of four generations (and at one time, five generations) with you, as I will be honored in Heaven. I cried so many tears while I was writing this book and putting all of the recipes on the pages. It has been the most rewarding project of my career, and I live every day to make you proud. This book, as well as every first small half-and-half cup of creamer for my coffee, is for you.

To the other two parts of our four generations: my Ninny and my Mom. You have also shaped me into the woman I am today, and I am thankful for you every day and for your guidance with this book. You are the best editors and role models I could ask for as I trek through my life's adventures.

To my other Guardian Angel, Theo Tippett. I made you a promise in seventh grade, and I am keeping it now. This first book is for you, the mentor who always believed in my writing skills and a successful future. I red-inked drafts of this book in your memory!

Foreword..1

"Eternal Violet"..3
"Granny's Porch"...9

Recipe Collections
- **I.**   Breakfast...11
- **II.** Dinner/Supper..15
- **III.** Dessert...37
- **IV.** Holiday Staples..49

Acknowledgments...57

Write In Other Recipes...58

Me, playing with Little People and Legos in Granny's upstairs bedroom closet (first one on the right), 1990s.

Foreword

Granny felt the most at home in a kitchen. The kitchen was her area of solace, happiness, and rumination. Even when the Roaring '20s transformed into the Great Depression, she kept her spirits up, her American Dreams alive, and her family fed. She cooked thousands of meals for her four children, husbands, parents, siblings, nieces, nephews—and everyone in the neighborhood. When the last August moon fell on Papaw Earl's life and through all of her life's transgressions, I am sure she sat at her kitchen table, talking to God and easing her troubles through cooking.

Nothing made her more proud than to make a meal for her grandchildren and great-grandchildren. Granny made any kitchen hers, whether it was part of one of her houses or if she was just visiting one of her loved ones. She didn't even have to cook in order for it to be illuminated with her love and passion for her family and cooking. Her stories and vibrant brown eyes lit up any room. She told me so many stories at her wooden kitchen table on 16th Street Road: The Great Depression, her children, Papaw Earl, her schoolhouse days, her hopes and dreams for me. She would sing as she stirred her latest batch of vegetable soup or used potholders to get hot, homemade cornbread out of the oven.

She showed her love for all of us in many ways, but food was a primary showcase of love. If she knew someone liked something, then that is what she made for that person. Summer days were filled with phone calls and voyages from her house to mine to bring me macaroni salad, lemon pies, and vegetable soup. And to this day, I will never taste biscuits and gravy like hers.

There will never be anyone like her. This compilation of her masterpieces in the kitchen will serve as the reminder of days gone by. These recipes, when available, are in their original formats. Although spelling and other terminology may differ from today's standards, I wanted to maintain the integrity of Granny's archives. With this book, all of us will keep her memory alive in our own kitchens.

So, here's my ode to our beloved Granny.

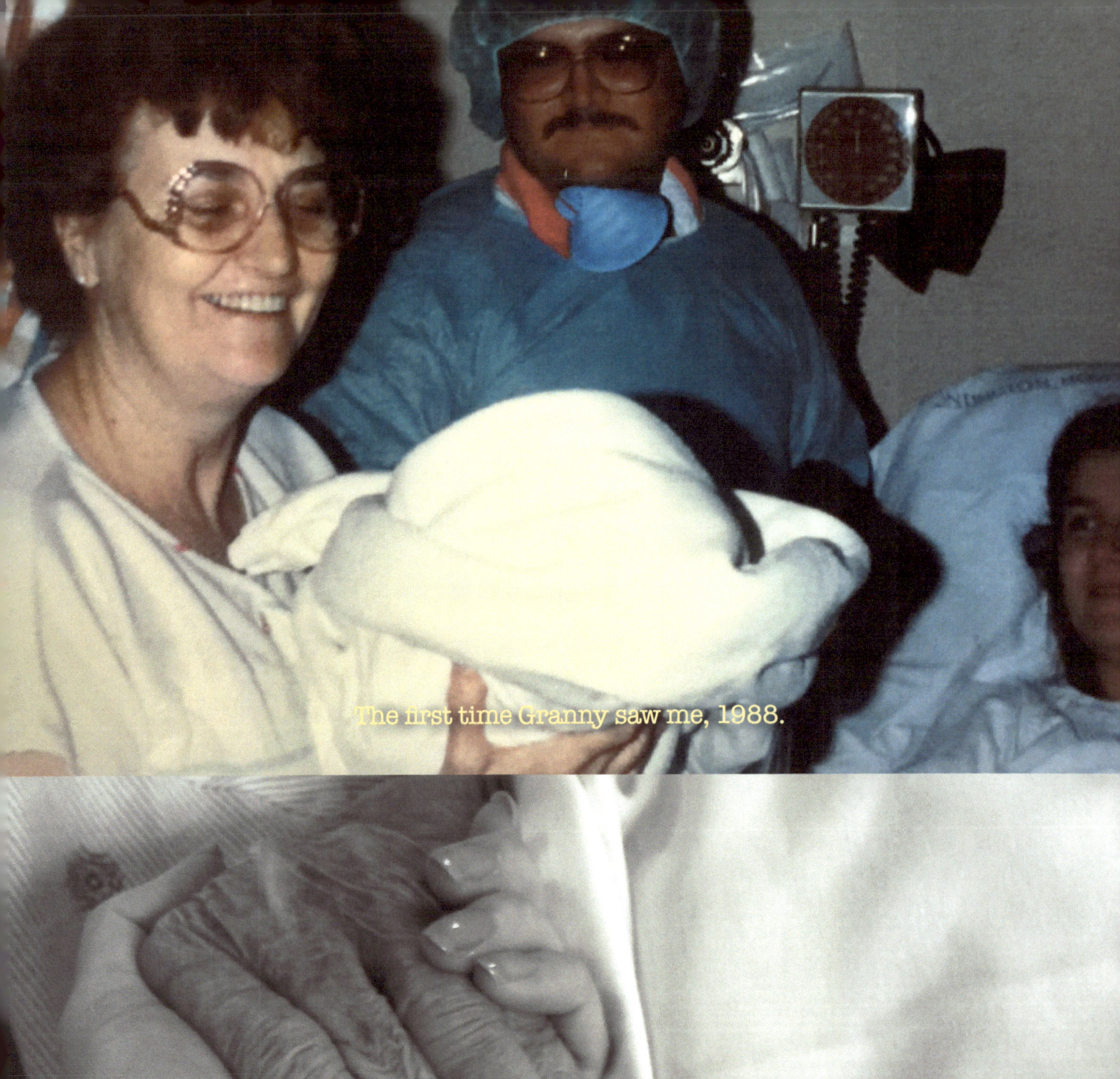

The first time Granny saw me, 1988.

Our last moments together, 2015.

"Eternal Violet"

I adjust my eyes to seemingly unfamiliar surroundings as I wipe the sleep from my eyes. For a moment, I forget where I am. Floral wallpaper greets my tired eyes, and a flood of pink trickles into my line of view. This isn't my serene blue oasis with the massive comfortable bed. A shot of pain shoots through my lower back as I move about. This bed is composed of nails, it seems. A car's tires shriek through the hairpin turn outside of the window as the humid summer rain hits the asphalt and windowpane. The bed is situated near the window, and I wish I could drown those sounds out of the thinly insulated walls.

The faint aroma of breakfast begins to envelop the room as I emerge from my slumber of a night full of tossing and turning. I catch a brief glimpse of a photo of me when I was in seventh grade in a frilly fabric photo frame. My eyeglasses seem to swallow my entire face with my oversized nose and awkward grin.

Where is the better photo of me—the one from elementary school? I wonder.

I presume it is behind the horrendous caricature that I eventually admit is myself. The digital clock on the circular mahogany table transmits the time onto the ceiling. I grab my less-invasive glasses and realize that it is nearly 11 a.m. I slept longer than I wanted to.

I sluggishly walk across the tan carpet and open the painted white door. I glance at myself in the tall mirror in the hallway near the stairs. Admiring the fact that I look skinny in my "Alice in Wonderland" pajamas, I venture into the bathroom and lock the door with the brass latch lock. The floor creaks as I head toward the sink, and I weigh myself on the scale sitting between the lavatory and commode. 107 pounds. As a 5'4" senior in high school, this seems like a low weight. Perhaps the stress of being the editor of the school newspaper is finally taking its toll.

I retrieve my toothbrush and toothpaste from my blue Paris-themed overnight bag and look toward the closed windows. I have always loved the hatch windows in this bathroom. When I was little, I opened the wooden doors on them from the inside and looked out into the world I hadn't fully explored yet. I watched the vehicles cross the double-yellow line as I sat perched on the

"Eternal Violet"

toilet seat. Then, I wasn't aware that people could actually see in those windows. I suppose I was under the impression they were two-way mirrors used in police interrogation rooms.

I descend the blue carpeted stairs—the ones Hannah and Will jumped down one Thanksgiving or Christmas. They leaped from the top and landed near the window at the bottom of the landing. They paid little regard to the fact that one or both of them could have crashed through the window and punctured themselves with the glass shards. No one seemed to pay attention, a rarity in my family.

On my trek to the kitchen, I pass by the oak coffee table, piled with a multitude of Good Housekeeping magazines and a wide-based vase of light blue and mauve faux flowers. When I was little, I opened the drawer and pretended it was a palace full of Little People and Legos. A blue, yellow, and red Lego staircase led to the roof, which was the entire expanse of the table.

Hannah sits at the kitchen table, a heap of gravy and biscuits on her white plate with a mustard-colored floral deco design around the perimeter. The crackling and sizzling of bacon slices into the accent-infused melody Granny is singing. She is singing a made-up song about Lucille not having any underwear again. She is at the stove, clad in a forest green short-sleeved sweater, gray slacks, and brown pantyhose. Her brown eyes meet my blue eyes, and she gently smiles.

She doesn't even have to say a word. Her expressive eyes say everything all at once, but she speaks anyway.

"Kay-Kay Renee, get yourself a plate and get some biscuits and gravy. There's the salt and pepper. Get yourself a fork," she says. "Do you want some bacon?"

My stomach grumbles, nearly answering her questions for me. I open the wooden cabinet over the microwave and get out a plate. My plate is white with a black diamond and pink floral design. I ladle some gravy onto two large biscuits from a can.

Thank goodness they're not the butter kind, I think, spoiled by the way Granny cooks breakfast. I pour myself a glass of milk, making sure to use a tall blue glass with the moons and stars on it. I notice Granny's small jelly glass near the sink. It's full of tap water, and she likely used it to take sips of water when she took her collection of medications earlier in the morning. The smell of fabric softener enters the kitchen from her small laundry room. I notice neat stacks of underwear, fitted sheets, and nightgowns on top of the dryer. She always washes everything together because her loads are so small.

"Eternal Violet"

Granny, Hannah, and I settle in and devour our breakfast. While I observe her laundry, Granny piles some scrambled eggs on my plate, too. I am glad I woke up in time to eat because biscuits and gravy are a weekly tradition for us. Granny tells us stories of Papaw Earl, rough times during the Great Depression, and being good at her studies at her one-room schoolhouse in Wayne County. We both intently listen, and when we're through, Granny washes the dishes. Hannah and I open the door to the front porch, greeted by a warm breeze and sounds from Wooten Machine Shop across the street. The rain showers have stopped, and the sun illuminates the hazy sky. We plop down on the light blue swing, talking and watching the traffic blurs go by.

I lose myself in thought. I'm seven years old with long brown hair, and Granny and I are piled on the same swing. My miniature legs and feet propel us to high magnitudes, ones that allow the swing to flutter above the concrete slab railing on the brick porch. The arches of my feet touch the brick wall, and I push us higher and higher. Although she is 67 years old, she doesn't seem to mind her first great-grandchild's antics and the creaking swing chain. She sings to me, a comforting lullaby in the back of my mind. Her curly dark hair rustles with the passing breezes, and for a moment, time stands still.

Then, the vision begins to fade back into reality. And just like that, it's gone in a flash. I climb behind the driver's seat of my dark green Toyota Camry, parked in the side yard where my favorite tree used to be: the one Granny had cut down because it was nearly coming down anyway. It was the one I used to play hide-and-seek behind and was upset about when I discovered one day it was gone. Hannah climbs in the passenger seat, and we're off. I avoided the the way the protective lining underneath my car would scrape when I tried to drive up the monstrous, concrete driveway. We head home until the next time we stay the night with Granny again. Before we leave, she reaches into her wallet and generously gives Hannah and me $5 apiece.

My naïveté prevented me from realizing a bitter truth: All of this vibrancy would inevitably turn to dust.

She isn't this person lying in the hospital bed in her den. It wasn't too long ago that she would sit here in her maroon recliner, talking about her meals of the day and watching Food Network when I picked up Hannah after she got off the bus there. Hannah would munch on a Hershey bar, and I would get a can of Sunkist out of her garage refrigerator.

This can't be her. The person who blacked out at the wheel and hit another car head-on that June afternoon, leaving her in intensive care for weeks. She

"Eternal Violet"

was almost home. She nearly made it back from her errands safely. She was almost home to her Lord, whose hands were reaching for her on the ambulance ride to the hospital. She was prodded with tubes and needles galore, yet God allowed her to remain here with us even after the darkest hour seemed to crumble the ounces of optimism within our breaking hearts. This can't be her because this woman's mind was never the same after that accident.

This can't be her. This person is decrepit with a sullen face like all of those seen on their deathbeds. A pink nightgown fits loosely on her body, which is all skin and bones now. Her wedding rings roll around on her left ring finger—the diamond never remaining in one place at any given time. Her hair is fully gray and wrinkles seem to be painted on her face with an old-age brush. Her speech is slurred due to the massive stroke that usurped her corollary artery and left side of her brain.

These can't be my tears streaming down my cheeks. This can't be me breaking down and sobbing in the shower, putting my hand to my heart—just like Professor Marvel told Dorothy that Aunt Em was doing when he gazed into his crystal ball. Although I'm in my 20s now, I sometimes clutch my stuffed Mowete (Shotgun Red in mainstream terms) at 2 a.m. and think of how Granny sewed some new pants for him when I ripped his original ones. She was in good health two years ago when she perused Ninny's rummage sales, cooked fried potatoes, watched court cases unravel on TV, and opened Christmas presents. Little did we know that 2008 would be the last normal year of her life.

This can't be how she will spend the remainder of her days on earth, trapped in this bed, clinging to what is left. This can't be my Granny.

It can't. It can't.

But, it is. I barely recognize her anymore. Even she doesn't know who she is anymore.

But, her eyes are the same, and I'm one of the lucky ones she still recognizes from time to time. She caresses my face and holds my hand, like she remembers the nights we stayed with her, the days spent on the swing, the food she fed me, the stories she told. It's almost as if she remembers getting the India ink stain out of my Candyland sweatshirt when I was in middle school. It's as if my brain transfers these images to her with one single touch. All I have left of her earthly body is a few understood words and her expressive eyes, the eyes that used to plead with me to sit and talk with her a while.

Does she remember the songs she used to sing? The endless amounts of

"Eternal Violet"

bubblewrap she would pop? The birthday cards she would send to her family? The Wednesdays and Fridays we would spend the night with her? The Fats Domino album she let me borrow and I always forgot to return? Does she remember all of those nights we watched "Dateline" specials on TV? Does she remember our mutual love for gummy worms? Does she remember getting out of her car to talk in the speaker in the Arby's drive-thru because they couldn't hear her?

This is the Granny who would stop by my old house after work to see me when I was a newborn. This is the Granny who bought me a "Lion King" electronic game at K-Mart when my mom wouldn't buy it for me. This is the Granny who fed my cat for us when we were on vacation, even though she honestly never liked animals that much. This is the Granny who delivered her homemade soup and lemon pies to us in her boat of a car. She is the Granny I drove to Gabriel Brothers with Hannah and who bought two new nightgowns and me some new socks and earrings. She is the Granny who always ordered fried flounder at Red Lobster and loved the breadsticks at Fazoli's, as well as my mom's tostadas. She is the Granny we affectionately called "Wanda the Witch."

All of the memories invade my mind, almost like framed photographs lining my walls or glass ornaments on her massive Christmas tree. They haven't lost their sparkling luster, and they never will be taken from me. No amount of defenseless denial will eradicate the truth. I grip the purple heart stone in the gold banded ring on my right middle finger, wishing I could give up anything to have those overnight stays back. The hard mattress, the loud traffic, the magical scale, the biscuits and gravy. I never realized how special those little moments were until they vanished from me, until she was gone that rainy July night in 2015.

She will never see me become the person I always wanted to be, the person with the illustrious career. She will never see me walk down the aisle on my wedding day or meet her great-great-grandchildren. She will never walk through the front door of my house. All I will have left are memories, which may eventually be enough to comfort me at night. Granny now resides in a mansion where she will never grow old, where the streets are paved in pure gold and pain does not inflict her. She can move her right side again, and her bad knee will be fixed. She has seen Papaw Earl and Charlie again, her two husbands she loved on this earth, and family members long gone. She lives with her Savior for eternity, and that fact will allow me to peacefully rest when the pain becomes too much to handle.

I grew up never gearing for the goodbye tears; my cares floated with the bygone breezes induced by Granny's front-porch swing. The rose-colored glasses are broken in pieces and scattered about the trails of my life; however, I won't be haunted with regret but will cherish each memory with careful detail. She is everything I will always wish I can be but will always come up short.

The baby blue eyes and roses grew in the spring. Summer's brash and blazing temperatures lent themselves to autumn's falling leaves and briskness. Eventually, winter's icy breath encompassed our own little world. Now, Granny is not in this world. Thus is the circle of life's seasons, but her legacy will live on within me.

I hope to tell stories of Granny to my own children someday. I'm sure—without a shadow of a doubt—that my Guardian Angel will make me biscuits and gravy when I make it home to Heaven someday. After all, we will have a lot of stories to tell each other and catching up to do. And this time around, I will drink coffee with her.

"Granny's Porch"

Cars of every color zoom past at colossal speeds
The summer breeze lifts my loose hair and spirits as I sit—
I pile on the faded light blue porch swing I love so much
And I bring my hopes and dreams with me.

Granny's country-folk-infused melodies put me at ease—
As I swing my legs to and fro, pushing us higher
The metal chains clink and clunk and I could fall if I would
But, I remain there, contented and pleased.

Time passes by so slowly there, but yet, I wonder where it has gone
As the paint chips and chains rust, I struggle to hold on
It's all different now—I'm older, and the songs are gone
But, I bring my hopes and dreams with me.

KRA, 2008.

Granny in her kitchen, 1950s.

I. Breakfast

Hannah sits at the kitchen table, a heap of gravy and biscuits on her white plate with a mustard-colored floral deco design around the perimeter. The crackling and sizzling of bacon slices into the accent-infused melody Granny is singing. She is singing a made-up song about Lucille not having any underwear again. She is at the stove, clad in a forest green short-sleeved sweater, gray slacks, and brown pantyhose. Her brown eyes meet my blue eyes, and she gently smiles.

She doesn't even have to say a word. Her expressive eyes say everything all at once, but she speaks anyway.

"Kay-Kay Renee, get yourself a plate and get some biscuits and gravy. There's the salt and pepper. Get yourself a fork," she says. "Do you want some bacon?" — Excerpt From: "Eternal Violet."

Recipes

Bacon Sandwiches
Biscuits and Gravy
Cocoa Syrup

Bacon Sandwiches

INSTRUCTIONS
1. Preheat a 9-inch skillet on low heat.
2. Fry 6-7 slices of bacon (or as many as desired) in the skillet. Turn as needed until cooked.
3. Place bacon on a plate. Serve three slices on toasted bread with mayonnaise (Granny used Miracle Whip), tomato, lettuce, salt, and pepper.

Back in Time: Granny would fry bacon in her favorite cast-iron skillet. She would also save her bacon grease to flavor gravy and other dishes.

Biscuits and Gravy: see next page.

Biscuits & Gravy

Gravy
INGREDIENTS

1	tablespoon bacon grease
1	tablespoon flour
1	cup milk
	salt and pepper, to taste

INSTRUCTIONS

Heat large pan on the stove, medium heat. Melt bacon grease and flour to make a rue. Then, pour one cup of milk into the rue, stirring to thicken the gravy. Add salt and pepper. Recipe feeds two people. Adjust the recipe to feed more than two people.

Biscuits
INGREDIENTS

2	cups flour
1	tablespoon baking powder
1	teaspoon salt
1/3	cup shortening
3/4	cup milk
2	tablespoons butter
1/4	cup flour

INSTRUCTIONS

1. In bowl, combine flour, baking powder, and salt.
2. Cut in shortening until mixture resembles coarse meal.
3. Add milk. Stir until blended.
4. Knead dough on floured surface until smooth.
5. Roll to 1/2" thickness. Cut with floured cutter.
6. Bake on ungreased baking sheet at 425° F for 12-15 min. (Yields 20.)

Back in Time: In the 1960s and 1970s, Granny rolled out her homemade biscuit dough, cutting them in perfect circles with the rim of small jelly glasses. She would also mix Tang orange powder and water; she would drink Tang out of the same jelly glasses.

Cocoa Syrup

INGREDIENTS

1 cup sugar
1 cup water
2 tablespoons cocoa

INSTRUCTIONS

Mix ingredients. Bring mixture to a boil on the stove until it bubbles. Stir a couple of times. Let boil for 5 minutes, until the mixture becomes more thick. Turn off burner and serve with biscuits.

Granny and her family at Grandma Wooten's house, early 1960s.

Granny and Ninny at Granny's house on the ridge, 1990s.

II. Dinner/Supper

Everyone enjoyed these staples of Granny's kitchen, and while they were all equally delicious, we have our favorites. For me, no one makes Mexican cornbread like Wanda V. Dean!

Recipes

Beans: Green, Pinto, White
Beets
Chili
Cornbread
Fried Green Tomatoes
Fried Potatoes
Homemade French Fries
Hot Dog Sauce
Mango Peppers
Mashed Potatoes

Meat Loaf
Mexican Cornbread
Roast and Vegetables
Salmon Cakes
Saucy Broccoli
Sauerkraut
Sauerkraut Salad
Spaghetti Sauce
Sweet Dill Pickles
Vegetable Soup

Beans: Green, Pinto, White

Green Beans
INGREDIENTS

1	teaspoon salt
1/4	cup cooking oil
1	slice of bacon

INSTRUCTIONS (For open-kettle cooking)
1. String and wash beans.
2. Place beans in pot.
3. Add water over beans 1/2" to 1."
4. Cook for 2 hours, to a hard boil.
5. Let water boil down.

Pinto Beans
INGREDIENTS

1	teaspoon salt
1/4	cup cooking oil
1	slice of bacon

INSTRUCTIONS (For open-kettle cooking)
1. Soak beans overnight. Place beans in a large pan of water.
2. The next day, cook 2 1/2 to 3 hours until soft.
3. Lower heat until beans are tender.

White Beans
INGREDIENTS

2	lb. bag of Great Northern beans
1	teaspoon salt
3/4	cup cooking oil
1	slice of bacon

INSTRUCTIONS (For open-kettle cooking)
Add water over beans 1/2" to 1." Cook to a hard boil for 1 hour.
Tip: Keep hot water handy to add so beans won't boil dry. Light pinto beans are also better than darker beans.

Beets

> Beet Receipt. July 29, 1980
> 2 cups Vinegar
> 1 cup Water
> 2 big tea cups sugar
> salt to taste a few mixed Spices
> bring to a boil drop Beets in
> Boil 10 or 15 minutes Put in Jars
> & seal while hot
>
> Written By
> Rita Adkins

Note: "Receipt" is an old-time way of spelling "Recipe."

4 Generations in the 1970s Mom, Granny, Geraldine, and Barbara

Chili

INGREDIENTS

1	64-ounce can tomato juice
1	large can kidney beans (undrained)
3-4	15-ounce cans pinto beans (undrained)
1	medium onion (peeled and diced)
2-3	tablespoons chili powder (or more, to taste)
1	pound of ground beef (optional; Granny made the soup with and without meat)

INSTRUCTIONS

1. If using ground beef, cook in a separate pan at this time, then drain grease.
2. Place kidney beans, pinto beans, diced onions, tomato juice, chili powder, and ground beef (if used) in a large pot.
3. Cook until boiling. Cover and simmer for about an hour.
4. Serve with crackers.

Granny at my parents' house, early 2000s.

Cornbread

INGREDIENTS

- 1 teacup of buttermilk (Granny used a Corelle® teacup)
- 1/2 teaspoon salt
- 2 tablespoons sugar
- 1 tablespoon flour
- 1 teacup of cornmeal
- 1 egg
- 2-3 tablespoons shortening

INSTRUCTIONS

1. Mix all ingredients. If the mixture is too thin, add more cornmeal. It should look like cake batter and not stiff like a brownie mixture.
2. Preheat the oven and place the empty pan with shortening (Crisco® is recommended) in the oven until hot and the shortening melts, coating the pan. Make sure pan is really hot before taking it out of the oven and putting the batter in.
3. Bake 15 minutes at high temperature: 400°F or 450°F.
4. To brown top, broil. Watch until brown.

Granny at her dining room table, 1970s.

Fried Green Tomatoes

INGREDIENTS

- 2-3 medium or large green tomatoes
- 1/2 cup bacon grease, Crisco®, or other cooking oil
- 1-2 cups cornmeal
- 1/4 cup flour
- 2 eggs
- 1 teaspoon sugar (optional)
- salt and pepper, to taste

INSTRUCTIONS

1. Wash and slice tomatoes. Preheat skillet with grease/oil on high heat.
2. Mix cornmeal, flour, salt, pepper, and sugar on a dinner plate.
3. Beat two eggs in a bowl.
4. Drop each green tomato slice in egg mixture and then coat with cornmeal/flour on both slides.
5. Fry tomatoes in skillet for 10 minutes or until brown on both sides.

Tip: Fry squash, eggplant, etc., the same way.

Having fun on vacation, 1980s.

Fried Potatoes

INGREDIENTS
- 6 medium or large potatoes
- 1/2 cup bacon grease, Crisco®, or other cooking oil
- salt and pepper to taste

INSTRUCTIONS
1. Wash, peel, slice, then cube potatoes. Put cubed potatoes in a large bowl. Preheat skillet with oil on high heat.
2. Pour potatoes in skillet and fry until the edges are brown and potatoes are tender. Put lid on to brown; cooking takes approximately 30 minutes.

Back in Time: Sometimes, Granny would also add onions to the fried potatoes. Geraldine liked them that way, but Roger and Randy liked them without onions.

A family gathering, 1960s.

Homemade French Fries

INGREDIENTS

6 medium or large potatoes (or a quantity to your liking)
1 entire can of Crisco® or another shortening

INSTRUCTIONS

1. Peel potatoes and slice to the thickness of your choice.
2. Heat shortening in a large open soup pot until boiling.
3. Cook potatoes until they're golden brown and drain on paper towels.
4. Put on a plate and serve.

Back in Time: Granny made endless batches of French fries when her children were growing up.

In the kitchen, 1960s.

Hot Dog Sauce

RECIPE: Hot Dog Sauce

From the Kitchen of:

1 lb. hamburger
1 med onion (brown together)
1 small can tomato paste
2 cans of water
½ cup Catsup
1 teaspoon of vinegar
1 tablespoon of Chili powder
1 teaspoon of garlic powder

1 teaspoon of salt
1 teaspoon of black pepper

Simmer for one hour or longer if desired

Granny with her four children (from left to right), Claude, Geraldine, Randy, and Roger, 1960s.

"Mango" (Banana) Peppers

Mango or Bananna peppers (Canning)

2 cups sugar
2 " Water
2 " Vinegar
Salt to taste - add mix spices
Combine all ingredients - bring to a boil
Add peppers a few minutes or until
Color changes. Put in cans & add
boiling solution. Then seal.

Note: Although the spelling is "mango," Granny would pronounce it "mingo." This is how it was pronounced back in Granny's day.

Mashed Potatoes

INGREDIENTS

8-10	medium or large potatoes
1	teaspoon vegetable oil
1	stick butter
1	5-ounce can evaporated milk
	salt and pepper, to taste

INSTRUCTIONS

1. Wash and peel potatoes. Cut potatoes into small chunks.
2. Cover potatoes with water in a pot. Cook with a teaspoon of oil so the water doesn't boil over. Cook potatoes until tender. (Stick a fork in a potato to see if it's done.)
3. Drain potatoes and mash with an electric mixer or potato masher. Pour in evaporated milk gradually. Fold in butter as you mix the potatoes.
4. Add salt and pepper to taste. Serve.

Me, enjoying a Thanksgiving meal, complete with mashed potatoes, 1990s.

Meat Loaf

1½ ground beef
½ cup mango peppers
½ cup chopped onions
2 eggs
½ cup ketchup
½ cup oats
1½ tablespoon brown sugar
salt & pepper to taste
mix together

{ ¼ cup brown sugar
⅓ " ketchup
½ cup water } pour over top

1 hr. 15 min. 350°

Mexican Cornbread

> **MEXICAN CORNBREAD**
>
> ½ cup oil
> 3 T. sugar
> 1 8oz. can cream corn
> ½ cup chopped onions
> ½ cup shredded cheese
> **1 egg***
>
> 1 cup sweet milk
> 1 cup flour
> 1 cup meal
> 1 sweet pepper
> 3 hot peppers or 3 banana peppers
>
> Bake at 350° for 30-60 minutes or until brown.

Tip 1:
Add Crisco® to the pan and let heat up in the preheated oven, until the Crisco® melts. Put just enough so it coats the pan. Watch so it doesn't burn.

Tip 2:
Granny never left her cornbread in the pan to serve. She flipped over the pan and put the cornbread on a Corelle® plate.

Note: These tips can also be used on the regular cornbread recipe.

*This was added after this recipe was tested.

Roast and Vegetables

INGREDIENTS
1	2 lb. boneless beef chuck roast
4-6	medium potatoes, cut into halves
1	bag baby carrots
1	cooking onion, sliced
	garlic salt or garlic powder, to taste
	salt and pepper, to taste

INSTRUCTIONS
1. Preheat the oven to 350°F.
2. Place the chuck roast in the center of an 9x13 glass or aluminum baking pan. Season with pepper, garlic salt/garlic powder. Cover with aluminum foil. Bake for 1 1/2 hours.
3. Turn chuck roast over on the other side and place peeled and sliced potatoes, carrots, and onions in pan with roast. (If roast seems dry, pour approximately 1/2 cup of hot water over the roast before placing vegetables in.) Season vegetables with salt and pepper.
4. Cover with aluminum foil and bake 1 more hour. (You may have to bake a little longer to make sure vegetables are tender.)
5. Serve with light bread (this is what Granny called sandwich bread).

Note: The chuck roast will be juicy and will give flavor to the vegetables.

Back in Time: "When I was younger, I would help Granny clean her house on Saturdays. She would fix a roast, and as I was cleaning, I would smell it baking in her kitchen at her house on the ridge. She also taught me how to make this."—Earlene Adkins (my mom and one of the editors of this book).

Granny and Mom at Red Lobster (one of Granny's favorite restaurants), 1990s.

Salmon Cakes

INGREDIENTS
- 1 can of salmon
- 1 egg
- 1 cooking onion
- 1/2 cup Crisco® shortening or vegetable oil
- 5-6 Saltine crackers, crushed
- salt and pepper, to taste

INSTRUCTIONS
1. Drain juice from can of salmon. (Save the juice, if needed, to moisten the mixture later.)
2. Mix egg, crushed Saltine crackers, onion, salmon, salt, and pepper with your hands. Flatten into patties. Add juice if it's too dry.
3. Add oil in skillet and preheat. Cook salmon cakes and fry on each side until brown. Takes approximately 30 minutes to fry all of the salmon cakes.

Back in Time: Granny would make her salmon cakes in an electric skillet in her garage—because she didn't want her entire house to smell!

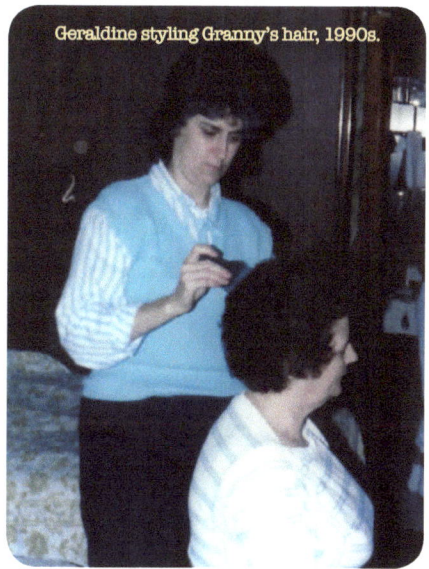

Geraldine styling Granny's hair, 1990s.

Saucy Broccoli

2 packages (10 ounces each) Thawed Frozen Broccoli Spears
½ cup Finely crushed Cheddar Cheese Crackers
1¼ cup (10¾ oz can) cream of Mushroom Soup
⅔ cup Undiluted carnation evaporated Milk
⅓ cup water
¼ cup Parmesan cheese
2 Tablespoons Instant minced Onions
⅛ Teaspoon pepper
2 Table Spoons Finely crushed Cheddar cheese crackers

Cook Broccoli according to package directions. drain place Broccoli in 10x6x2-inch Buttered Baking dish. Sprinkle ½ cup crushed crackers over Broccoli. Combine Soup, evaporated milk, water, Cheese, onions and pepper in Medium bowl. Pour over broccoli. Sprinkle Two Tablespoons crushed Crackers over Top. Bake in Moderate 350-degree oven 20 to 25-minutes or until bubbly and heated through. Makes 6-8 Servings

Written by
Beatrice Wooten
Sept 28, 1993

Sauerkraut

INGREDIENTS

1   can store-bought sauerkraut (or 1 quart of home-canned sauerkraut)
1/2   cup vegetable oil
      optional: sausage or hot dogs (sliced)
      salt and pepper, to taste

INSTRUCTIONS

1. Drain sauerkraut.
2. Preheat oil in skillet. Fry sauerkraut on high heat until it's cooked through. Stir often because it will burn easily. It changes color when done.

Tip: Add sausages or hot dogs as the sauerkraut is frying.

Four of five generations, 1990s.

Sauerkraut Salad

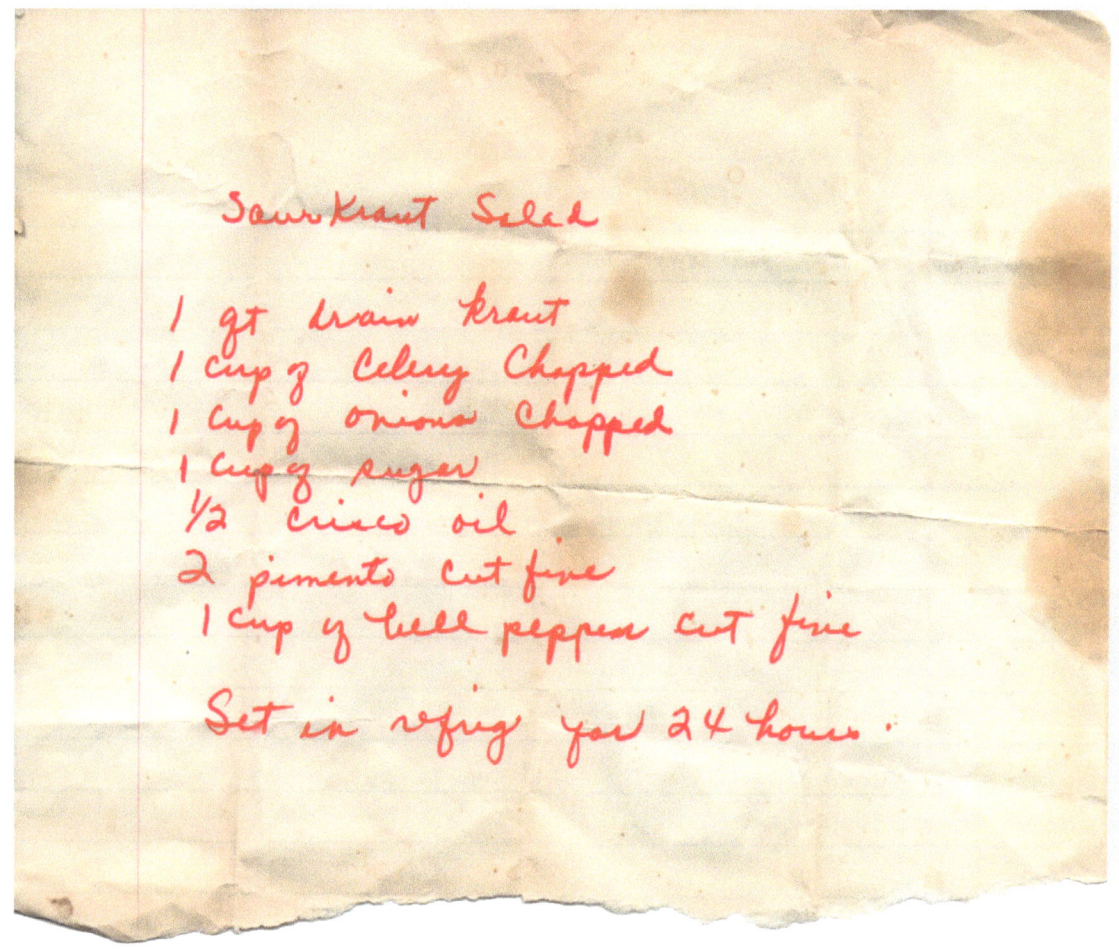

Sauerkraut Salad

1 qt drain kraut
1 cup of Celery Chopped
1 cup of onions Chopped
1 cup of sugar
½ Crisco oil
2 pimento cut fine
1 cup of bell pepper cut fine

Set in refrig for 24 hours.

Spaghetti Sauce

Spaghetti Sauce

2 lb. hamburger
salt & pepper to taste
1 T sugar
1 mango pepper chopped up
1 med. onion
1 T chili powder
garlic salt to taste
1 small bottle ~~little~~ catsup 14oz.
~~1 small tomato juice~~
1 small can tomato juice 24oz.
simmer two hrs.

Spaghetti dinner at Earlene and Jeff's (my parents') house, 1990s.

Sweet Dill Pickles

Sweet Dill Pickles
1 quart dill pickles drained
quartered or sliced.
3 cups sugar - 1 cup Vinegar
2 Tbls pickling spice
Boil Sugar, Vinegar & Spices
5 min.
strain and cover over
pickles back in Jar.
cool, cover and Refrigerate
12 hrs. before Serving.
These pickles are crisp
and Very good.

Back in Time: Granny also made sweet pickles and onions, canning them for the winter months.

Vegetable Soup

INGREDIENTS

1	64-ounce can of tomato juice
3	medium potatoes, peeled and sliced
3-4	carrots, peeled and sliced
1	medium onion, peeled and sliced
1	can of peas, undrained
1	can of corn, undrained
1	small head of cabbage, shredded (you can use half or all)
1	tablespoon sugar
1	pound of ground beef (optional; Granny made the soup with and without meat)
	salt and pepper, to taste

INSTRUCTIONS

1. Place potatoes, carrots, onions, and cabbage in a large pot. Cover vegetables and place lid on pot. Boil vegetables until tender.
2. If using ground beef, cook in a separate pan at this time, then drain grease.
3. After the vegetables are tender, drain approximately 1/2 of the water left in the pot. Add peas, corn, ground beef (if used), salt, pepper, tomato juice and sugar to the vegetables.
4. Bring soup to a boil. Cook and simmer for at least 1 hour.
5. Serve with peanut-butter sandwiches and crackers.

Back in Time: Granny would cut all of her vegetables—and anything, really—with her infamous butcher knife.

Granny in Tyler's dorm room, 1990s. She always traveled to visit her children, grandchildren, and great-grandchildren.

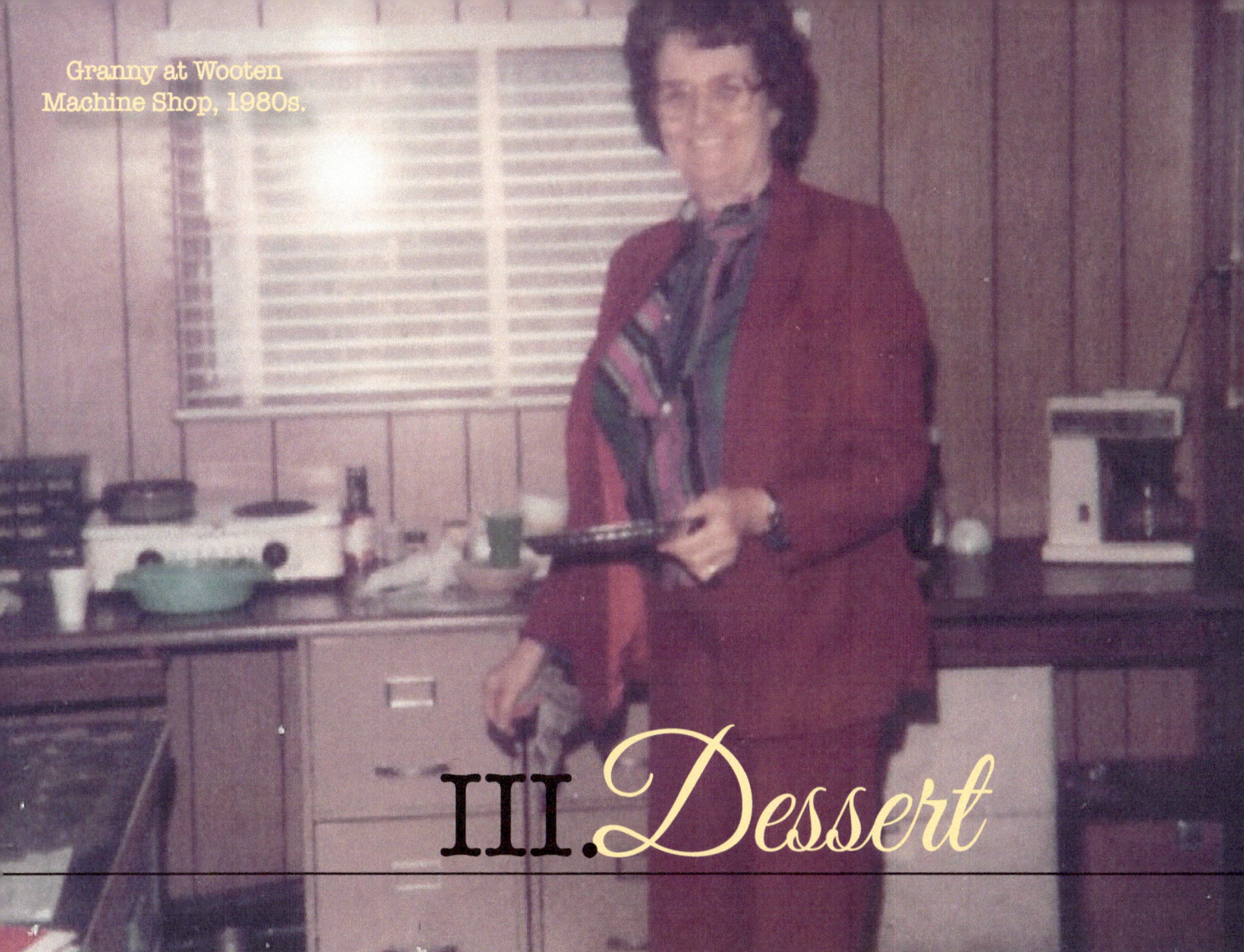

Granny at Wooten Machine Shop, 1980s.

III. Dessert

At least once a week, Granny would drive to my house to bring me a collection of cooked goodies. The majority of the time, she would call me to tell me she had made me a lemon pie. Of course, she never put Cool Whip on it because she knew I preferred it plain. And every time I taste Peach Jell-O, I step back into a time machine, when she made it at Ma and Pa's house in the 1990s.

Recipes

Apple Bread
Blackberry Cake
Bread Pudding
Cranberry Tea
Cream Cake
Fresh Apple Cake

Fresh Cobbler
Hot Cocoa
Lemon Cake
Pie Crust with Fillings
Pineapple Cherry Cake

Apple Bread

1 C oil
3 eggs
2 TS vanilla
3 C flour
1/2 tea salt
2 C sugar
2 C chopped tart apples — line pan
1 tea soda
1 C chopped nuts   8 oz

350 - 50 - 60

Combine eggs, sugar, oil, vanilla
add apples, combine dry ingred.
and add with nuts.
Bake in ungreased loaf
pans 350° 50-60 or until
toothpick comes out clean

Blackberry Cake

Black Berry Cake

- 3 eggs well beaten
- 2/3 stick butter
- 1 1/2 cups sugar
- 1 cup Jam
- 1 cup sour milk
- 3 cups plain flour
- 1 teas. cinnamon
- 1/2 ts. cloves
- 1/3 teas. salt
- 1 teas. vanilla
- 1 teas. soda
- 1 teas. Baking P.

400 degree
30 min.

Granny at my high-school graduation party at my parents' house, 2006. She always had her "swiping rag" (tissue) and a cup of coffee.

Bread Pudding

Bread Pudding
2 cups bread crum (about 3 Slices)
3 eggs
½ cup sugar
¼ Teaspoon Salt
1⅔ Cups evaporated Milk
1 cup Boiling water
½ Teaspoon Vanilla
1 Teaspoon Lemon peel graded
1 cup raisins

over

Place bread in a Buttered Baking dish
Beat the eggs and add Sugar, Salt &
Milk, stir in Vanilla & Lemon peel
Pour over bread Bake at 350
degrees until set at about 45 minutes

(For a larger receipt you may
double this one)

Cranberry Tea

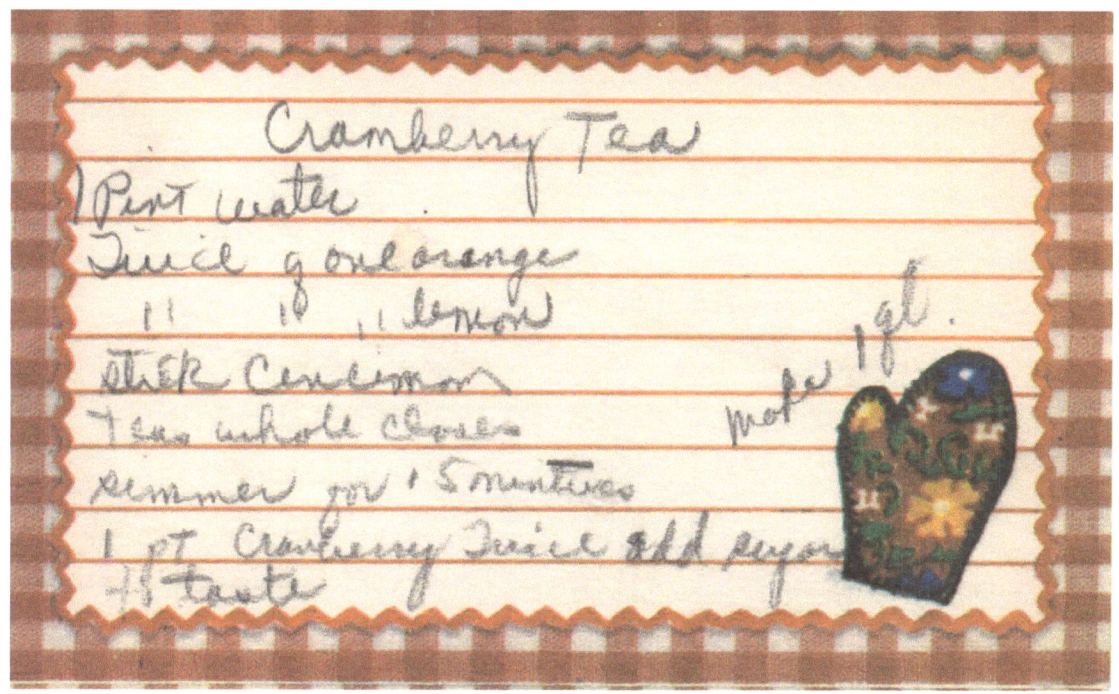

Cranberry Tea
1 Pint water
Juice of one orange
" " " lemon
Stick Cinnamon
7 or so whole Cloves
make 1 qt.
Simmer for 15 minutes
1 pt Cranberry Juice add sugar
to taste

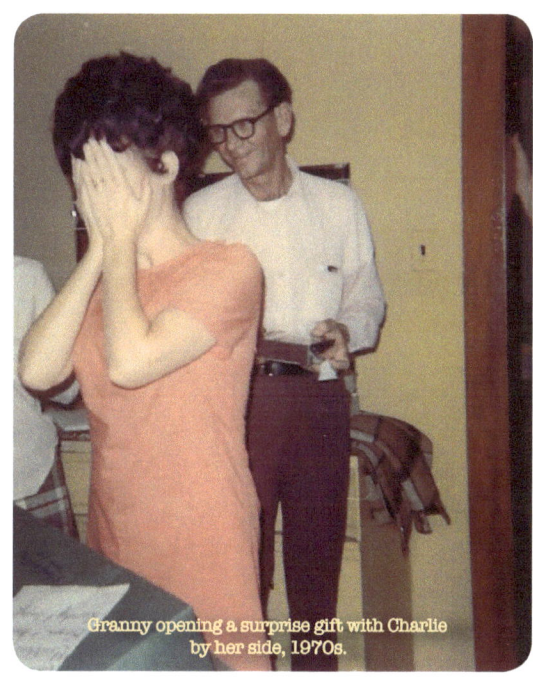

Granny opening a surprise gift with Charlie by her side, 1970s.

Cream Cake

Cream Cake

1 pk. Duncan Hines Pineapple Supreme Cake mix
1/2 C. Crisco oil
1 pkg. Vanilla or pineapple instant pudding
4 eggs — 1 C. water

Blend together & beat for 2 min
Bake in greased & floured 10" tube pan
350° for 45 to 55 min

For Glaze — mix 1 C. sifted powdered sugar
2 tablespoon milk.

Pineapple — Choc. or — Spice

Geraldine (Ninny) at Granny's dining-room table, 1970s.

Fresh Apple Cake

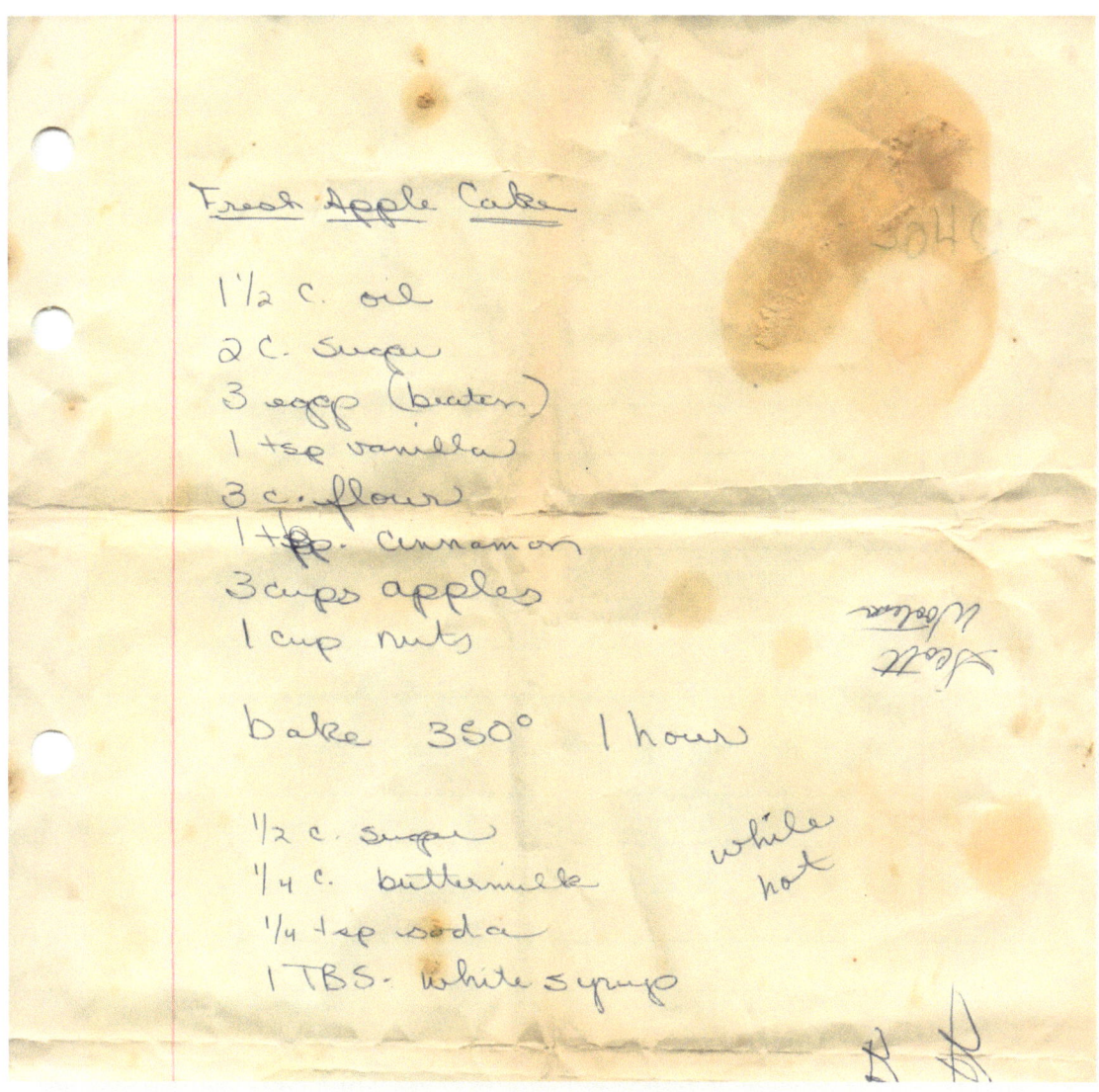

Fresh Apple Cake

1 1/2 c. oil
2 c. sugar
3 eggs (beaten)
1 tsp vanilla
3 c. flour
1 tsp. cinnamon
3 cups apples
1 cup nuts

bake 350° 1 hour

1/2 c. sugar
1/4 c. buttermilk
1/4 tsp soda
1 TBS. white syrup

while hot

Back in Time: Granny always made this in a Bundt-cake pan.

Fresh Cobbler

Fruit Cobbler

3/4 cup sugar
3/4 cup flour
3/4 cup milk
1 teaspoon baking powder
1 teaspoon salt

Melt ½ stick margarine (8 x 8 x 2) in pan. Pour batter into melted butter

2 cups of fruit + 2/3 cup sugar, mix together then sprinkle over batter. Bake in 400° oven for 40 minutes

Hot Cocoa

Hot Cocoa

1/4 cup + 2 Tablespoons of cocoa

1/2 cup sugar

dash of salt

4 cups of milk

Mix cocoa, sugar & salt in a saucepan

Add small amount of the milk (about 1/3 cup) and stir to form a smooth paste.

Stir in remaining milk. Heat thoroughly! Do not boil.

Remove from heat & beat with rotary beater until foamy

Yield: 4-5 servings

Back in Time: Granny didn't really like instant hot chocolate, so she continued to make hot chocolate this way throughout the years. She would heat up the milk in a little saucepan.

Lemon Cake

Lemon Cake.
1 Box Yellow Cake Mix
1 " Lemon Jello
1 Cup of Warm Water
1 Cup of Wesson Oil
1 T Lemon Juice
3 eggs.
Mix - Bake 350° 30 minutes
9 X 13 pan
   Glaze - Prick Cake when warm
2 Cups Confectionary Sugar
mix with lemon juice
spread on warm cake

Pie Crust with Fillings

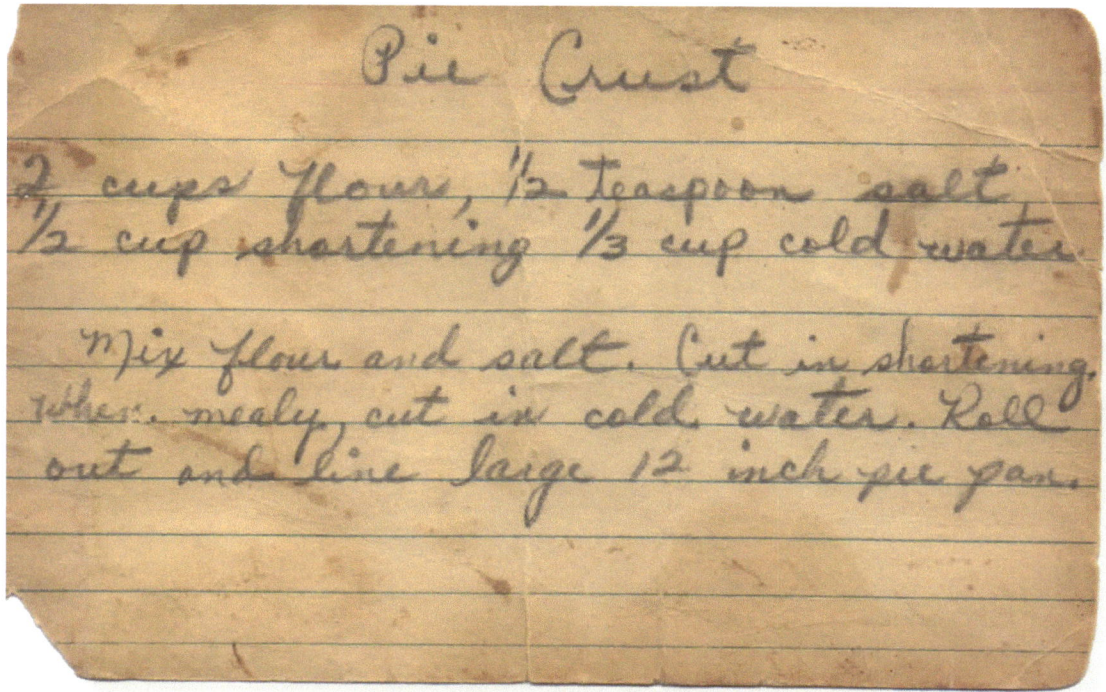

Note:
Granny would buy cook-and-serve chocolate and lemon gelatin JELL-O mixes and use them as fillings in her pies.

Granny telling me behind-the-scenes stories of photos at her 80th birthday party, 2007.

Pineapple Cherry Cake

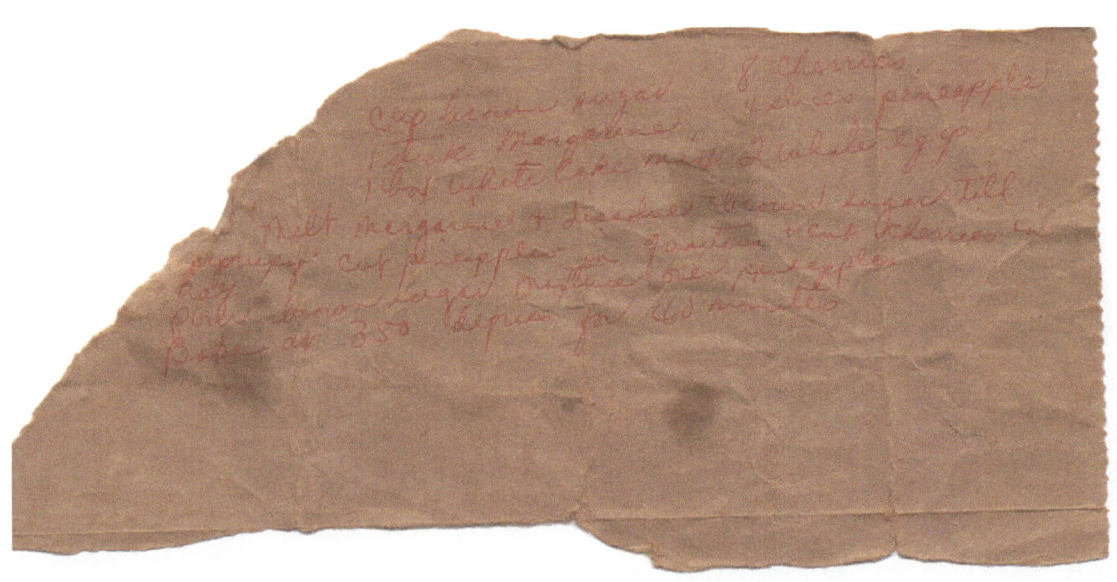

With Earlene and Todd, 1970s.

Granny at her July 4th celebration, 2008.

IV. Holiday Staples

Our family came together each Thanksgiving and Christmas—and most of the time, throughout the year on other special occasions. Each event boasted its own homemade foods from family members, but Granny made sure to have her "holiday staples" on the table at each special occasion.

Recipes

Cole Slaw
Cucumbers and Onions
Macaroni Salad
Potato Salad
Sweet Potatoes
Turkey Gravy

Cole Slaw

INGREDIENTS

1/2   head of cabbage, chopped
3   tablespoons mayonnaise (Granny always used Miracle Whip)
3   heaping tablespoons sugar
2   tablespoons vinegar

INSTRUCTIONS

Mix ingredients. Add pepper to taste. Then refrigerate.

Cole slaw.

Cucumbers and Onions

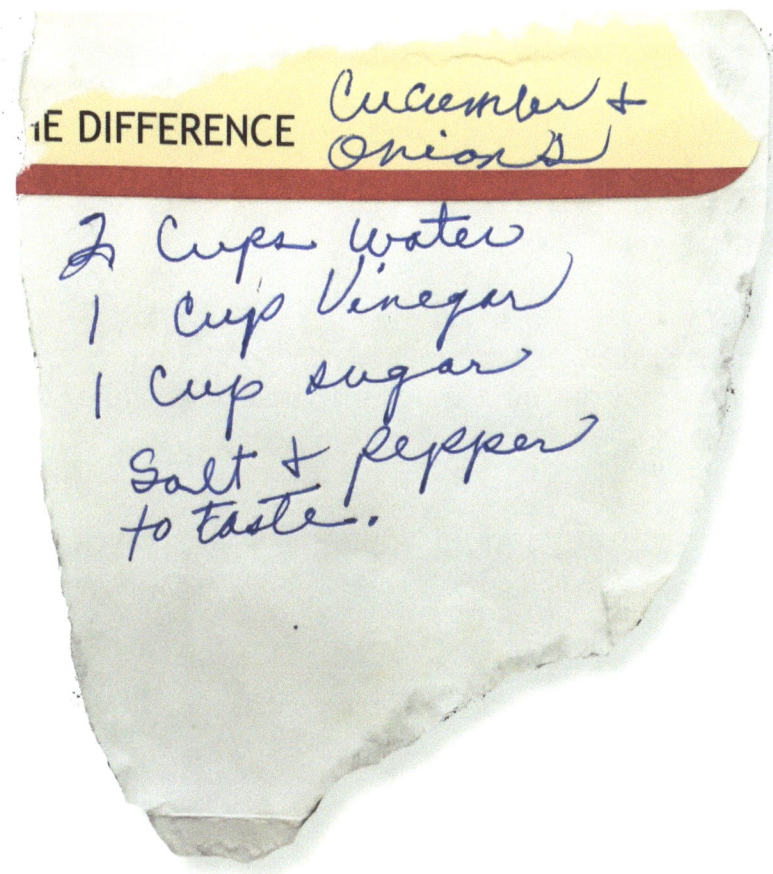

INSTRUCTIONS
Mix ingredients and refrigerate overnight. Then, serve.

Macaroni Salad

INGREDIENTS
- 2 cups of cooked elbow macaroni
- 1 1/2 cups mayonnaise, estimated (Granny always used Miracle Whip)
- 1 tablespoon mustard
- 1 cup sweet pickles, diced
- 3 teaspoons sweet pickle juice
- 5 cubed hard-boiled eggs

INSTRUCTIONS

Cook pasta and mix all ingredients. Then refrigerate.

Tip: Put 1 teaspoon cooking oil in water with macaroni while cooking to avoid noodles sticking together.

Ninny (Geraldine) and me at Granny's house, 1990s.

Potato Salad

INGREDIENTS

4-5	potatoes
1	teaspoon cooking oil
5	cubed hard-boiled eggs
1	cup sweet pickles, diced
3	teaspoons, sweet pickle juice
1 1/2	cups mayonnaise, estimated (Granny always used Miracle Whip)
1	tablespoon mustard

INSTRUCTIONS

Boil the potatoes. Add the cooking oil to water before potatoes are cooked. After potatoes are cooked, cool and then cut into cubes. Mix all ingredients. Cut up one hard-boiled egg for decoration. Then refrigerate.

Potato salad.

Sweet Potatoes

INGREDIENTS

2   large sweet potatoes
1   stick butter
     brown sugar (to sprinkle on top)
     pancake syrup (to sprinkle on top)

INSTRUCTIONS

Wash and cut sweet potatoes into halves or fourths. Boil sweet potatoes until tender. Place potatoes in a 13x9 dish and pour water in the bottom so the potatoes won't stick. Sprinkle butter, brown sugar, and syrup on the top of the potatoes. Bake 1/2 hour until brown.

Granny with some of her great-grandchildren, 2000s.

Turkey Gravy

Gravy
INGREDIENTS
- 1 tablespoon bacon grease
- 1 tablespoon flour
- 2 cups turkey broth or drippings from holiday turkey
- salt and pepper, to taste

INSTRUCTIONS
Heat large pan on the stove, medium heat. Melt bacon grease and flour to make a rue. Then, pour 2 cups of turkey broth or drippings into the rue, stirring to thicken the gravy. Add salt and pepper. Recipe feeds two people. Adjust the recipe to feed more than two people.

Granny at Geraldine's house, 2000s.

Wanda Violet Adkins Wooten Dean
"GRANNY"
1927-2015

Acknowledgments

Thank you to everyone who contributed to the making of this cookbook. I would like to extend an enormous thank you to my two editors, my Ninny and my mom. Without them, I couldn't remember and tweak each detail. Without Granny's attention to detail and her nostalgic tendencies, I wouldn't have had the recipes, photos, and memories to include in this book!

All photos were either taken by me (Kaylin R. Adkins) or provided by Granny's family, with permission to use for this publication. All stories and poems are Copyright © 2016 Kaylin R. Adkins, Hourglass Omnimedia, LLC.

[1] The "Wizard of Oz" quote on the dedication page and back cover are used via public domain under the Copyright Term Extension Act (CTEA), 1998, in the United States. In addition, all brand names are used with their registered trademarks. I do not own them.

Learn more about the publisher here!

ABOUT

KAYLIN R. ADKINS

Kaylin R. Adkins is an award-winning writer, photographer, and public relations practitioner from Huntington, WV. She graduated with her B.A. in public relations from Marshall University in 2010, and she is the owner of her own business, Hourglass Omnimedia, LLC. She loves Paris, but the Jewel City will always have her heart. This is her first "official" published book. She wrote her first compilation of stories when she was 7 years old.

Write In Other Recipes

Write In Other Recipes

Write In Other Recipes

Write In Other Recipes